Second Rain

SECOND RAIN

POEMS BY
Elise Hempel

ABLE MUSE PRESS

Able Muse Press

www.ablemusepress.com

Printed in the United States of America

Library of Congress Control Number: 2015955771

ISBN 978-1-927409-73-2 (paperback)
ISBN 978-1-927409-74-9 (digital)

Cover image: "Rainbow Daze" by Alexander Pepple

Cover & book design by Alexander Pepple

Able Muse Press is an imprint of *Able Muse:* A Review of Poetry, Prose & Art—at www.ablemuse.com

Able Muse Press
467 Saratoga Avenue #602
San Jose, CA 95129

for Ray, Bruce, Ed, and Ann

Acknowledgments

I am grateful to the editors of the following journals where many of these poems originally appeared, sometimes in earlier versions:

Angle: "I Know Now Heaven"

Blue Heron Review: "Night Exposure"

Blue Unicorn: "Preparations"

Borderlands: Texas Poetry Review: "On Butterfield Road"

Bottomfish: "The Guard"

Mezzo Cammin: "Stranger at a Cajun Funeral"

Snakeskin: "Projects," "Gravity," "Wood Thrush"

Spoon River Poetry Review: "The Soloist"

The Road Not Taken: "Elegy on Cleaning Day," "The Visitation"

The Rotary Dial: "The Church on Woodlawn," "Houdini's Girl," "Fledgling," "The Service"

Tar River Poetry: "Tablets," "Tigers at the Feline Rescue Center"

Valparaiso Poetry Review: "Today's Mail"

Foreword

In a manuscript copy of her new book she'd recently sent me, Elise Hempel had written, "I *hate* this poem" next to "The Yellow Phone" and had included two other poems to replace it, asking me to choose one of those instead.

"But neither is as good as what you have," I wrote back. "Keep 'The Yellow Phone'; it's your book in miniature."

"But it's so sentimental," she responded, and I thought back to a class I'd taught many years ago that Elise was in and the discussion we all had about sentimentality. I'd brought in some pretty sappy examples full of clichés that made for more laughs than tears, so I next tried some poems that risked no feeling at all, that read like language games, and the room fell silent. "These leave me cold," said the kid in a Cubs cap at the back of the room. "I'd rather read the weepy stuff."

I then passed around a copy of John Updike's poem "Dog's Death," which has all the potential for an overload of feeling: the death of a puppy as its owners hurry to the vet in an attempt to save the little dog. There wasn't a dry eye (mine included) in the classroom when I finished reading the poem. "But why isn't this poem sentimental," I asked, and so we began a productive discussion of Updike's diction, starting with the title itself where the dog remains anonymous ("Good thing he didn't call it 'Snoopy,'" one kid said!). We also looked at how Updike's syntax varied and how he shaped his stanzas with their hardly-noticed, subtle end rhymes. So, we concluded, maybe it's not the subject but how the language is used that makes a poem sentimental.

Where those budding young poets are now and what they might remember from our time together, I have no idea—except for one of them, that is, whose first full-length book I am honored to introduce. But first a word about Elise Hempel herself, someone I have known now for over thirty-five years as both a student and a friend.

Whether in a literature or writing class, her curiosity and insights singled her out as special, but her ability to shape her feelings into words remains what I find most unique, as have countless poetry editors around the country as well as the judges for the Illinois Arts Council. As editor of *The Spoon River Poetry Review* a few years ago, I nominated one of Elise's poems for a very competitive IAC award that year, and sure enough, she came away with first-prize and a thousand bucks in her pocket. And now along comes her first full-length collection from the well-respected Able Muse Press where Elise's *Second Rain* was a finalist, and rightly so, in their annual book contest.

From the opening title poem on, this is a book about the often ignored, simple gifts that come to us, like "the second rain that comes/ when the first is over," that "gentle scattering of drops" the breeze shakes down from the trees and "briefly blesses you." And similarly in "Today's Mail," the very next poem, we discover another such gift among the burden of "credit card bills and catalogs" at the bottom of the box, where the poet also finds "the crisp gleam/ of a June-bug's carapace":

> . . . this olive-
> brown gem, six black legs
> frozen in final flight
> or climb, wings like church doors
> arched and perfectly shut,
> this little weightless messenger

telling me today I owe
nothing, I'm fine as is,
this postcard from the wind, no
return address.

There are many of these "weightless messengers" in this book
of small blessings, such as in "Song in Mid-February," where "a
single bird somewhere/ ignores the biting air/ and sings its soft/
. . . sweet solo." Or in "The Guard" where amid the bulldozers
"shoving/ field into mall . . . this egret [is] still/ standing in its
pond . . . locked there." So much depends upon them, Elise Hempel
is suggesting, and in no poem does she do so more poignantly
than in "Tablets," with its touching first lines:

All through childhood I never quite knew what my
father did, when he left in pressed shirt, a tie,
driving somewhere with his lunch bag each morning, alone . . .

But what he brought home is where all of Elise's poems really
began:

. . . the drawing tablets he'd bring, those stacks
tucked under his arm on his way through the back
door at six—the slick, red, waxy spines
we'd run our fingers along, crack open to find
the wide new sheets with no rules, so white they'd glow,
our crayons setting out wherever we wanted to go.

And please look again at these lines I just quoted, at how they
end: each pair of them couplets so beautifully enjambed that we
never notice, these small miracles of craft.

    Which brings us somehow back to "The Yellow Phone" and
why it belongs in this book, Elise. That toy phone was just like
those drawing tablets your father brought home, and the crayons
you used on them was like your voice on that fake little thing

"connected/ to nothing but air." But "press the soft/ receiver to [your] ear," and you could call anyone, anywhere, just as you and we do in these wonderful poems.

Bruce Guernsey
Distinguished Professor Emeritus
Eastern Illinois University

Contents

Second Rain

Second Rain

I like the second rain that comes
when the first is over and
there's just enough left of the wind
to shake the trees all down
Whippoorwill Street, how as you step
beneath each one, a new
gentle scattering of drops
briefly blesses you.

Today's Mail

Just the crisp gleam
of a June-bug's carapace
I pulled from the bottom
of my near-empty box

that's usually stuffed with
credit-card bills and catalogs,
but today just this olive-
brown gem, six black legs

frozen in final flight
or climb, wings like church doors
arched and perfectly shut,
this little weightless messenger

telling me today I owe
nothing, I'm fine as is,
this postcard from the wind, no
return address.

Catalog

Though my mother never lived here, it arrives
in my mailbox today, another spring, her name
on the label above my address, this store she must have
ordered from at least once, the styles the same

each April: a Venice-scene dress with gondoliers
on the Grand Canal, another with a rose
or jungle print, a blouse with ruffles and tiers.
And still no models, just the empty clothes

floating on the pages, and I see her
getting ready again in this turquoise
jewel-trimmed top, now taking up this lavender
paisley purse, this sweater embroidered with dragonflies

in a world beyond illness, where nothing's plain or gray,
forever in her songbird earrings and her comfort
floral slides, waving as she sways
out to the endless luncheon in her rainbow skirt.

The Soloist

Inside this lidded sky
on the dining-room table,
above a fistful
of grass and leaves, one rock,
a katydid hugs the slant
of a dropped-in stick,
plucked from its part
in the afternoon's chorus, still

trilling alone
through the glass dusk in this made
field she left here,
my sisterless daughter, drifting
to the jar of her room where I've placed
one dresser, one bed,
another sunset humming
her single green song.

First Visit

After her stroke, half
of her body gone numb, my grandmother could
still muster up a sneer
at the hospital's cooking, dismiss
with a lumbering sweep of her hand
the mashed potatoes on her tray.

And she could still say
a few slow and muffled words,
though like someone in pain
who begins to speak
in their original tongue, forgetting
their second language, time and place,
she asked my father, aunt, and me
for my older brother, she
asked where the baby was.

Projects

The two pools he built and skimmed each day
with his net before work, his shirtsleeves rolled;
the basketball hoop he put up in the driveway,
sealing in creosote its wooden pole.

Or the skating rink that winter he froze
most of our yard, standing each night
in the cold dark for hours, the garden hose
in one hand, and in the other his flashlight

to ice our tracks smooth by morning—those efforts
that always came with his grunts and sighs,
his mumbled attacks on himself when the parts
didn't fit, his curses, then endless advice

and cautions afterward, trying to teach
the dangers of what he'd just made, a weight
I've long since lifted to see underneath
the gifts of a swim, the ball's swish, my figure eights.

Otto's Song

Potato chips must have been on sale
at the Kmart, or maybe nuts,
the Caddy tuned and getting its
miles per gallon, starting well.

Or maybe he'd just found
some better route and saved five minutes,
or he'd cleaned the gutters, fixed the furnace,
his stocks were up, or gas was down

that day I was on the sofa and he
walked in after Grandma, spoke for once
what wasn't a fact, some adage, a price,
when Elton John's "Your Song" happened to be

playing on our stereo, and the needle
suddenly skipped and lifted from
the constant march that played inside him
and he sang, almost, *That's beautiful.*

Song in Mid-February

It's three degrees with snow
on every roof that now
seems fixed in white refusal
to thaw, and through the dull
bare gray of early light,
as though born overnight,
a single bird somewhere
ignores the biting air
and sings its soft yet bold
sweet solo, new yet old,
against your aches and griefs,
returns a vague and brief
desire for what's ahead:
to gladly rise from bed.

Stranger at a Cajun Funeral

Too many names for me to comprehend,
my partner's family sprawling, unlike mine.
And when the Rosary comes my lips pretend
to speak the endless prayers. My hands are lost,
stay stiff and still while others glide the sign
of the cross with ease along their chests.
But I know the laughter mixed with tears
later at Jill's house, suits and dresses now
T-shirts and jeans, and all the bowls and platters
unwrapped, the bottles of whiskey and wine. And how
it's like a prayer when Don heads quietly out for
a smoke and Uncle Elbert deems the bread
pudding sweet enough with nothing more
than closing his eyes, one slow nod of his head.

Anagrams

Oh, if loss and failure really could
be turned around to *rainfall douses* instead,
and with a sturdy umbrella we could march
right through untouched,

and if genuine
death and grief, not just those words, could be proven,
with one brief stir, some *deranged faith*
we must never believe,

if when we're left or lost we could
simply pull two *linen soles*
from loneliness and slip
through its empty chill,

if, in a mere few seconds, *a spider*
with its steady resolve could be
woven from despair.

Gravity

The Ledge at Willis Tower, Chicago

To step from the concrete
floor to one of glass
and see beneath my feet
the moving cars, to pass

so quickly from solid to air
and float above the city,
to trust the brackets, enter
weightlessness from gravity

and leave the tower behind
with worry yet relief,
to stand up here and find
less doubt than belief

and know the soul before
my body must step back,
to momentarily hover
between faith and fact.

Elegy on Cleaning Day

Still, at the end, each morning, my mother got ready
in bright fluorescence, before the bathroom mirror,
primping for her day of naps, TV,
even as she saw her ever-thinner
face, putting on a little lipstick, a dab
of powder, unrolling the big rollers that gave
some semblance of shape to her hair, a fly-away web,
spraying her invisible helmet in circling waves.
Then made her way to the blue sofa in these
twin beige boats a decade in my closet,
still side-by-side, pointing outward, as she always
docked them next to the end table to await
each dwindling foot's insertion, her push—ten polished
ripples hard as stone, refusing to vanish.

I Know Now Heaven

I know now Heaven isn't up but down
and through a hidden battered door each night—
no clouds, just smoky air, a saxophone
billowing, falling, in the soft blue light.
I know now how to get there—just descend
the narrow winding stairs and feel my way
along the walls of brick, turn left around
another wall that's splattered with graffiti.
And there it'll be—a beer already at
my place at the nicked round table, and my mother
waiting again with hers to simply chat.
And when another set begins, once more
the ashtray is full, I need to wake and rise:
no need for tears, and only brief good-byes.

Tablets

All through childhood I never quite knew what my
father did, when he left in pressed shirt, a tie,
driving somewhere with his lunch bag each morning, alone,
the crunch of his tires in the driveway, coming home.
And though I know now what a graphic artist is
and where he went, a drafting board in an office,
I can only guess his doubts between money and dreams,
why he never ventured beyond that daily routine.
But I'm sure of the drawing tablets he'd bring, those stacks
tucked under his arm on his way through the back
door at six—the slick, red, waxy spines
we'd run our fingers along, crack open to find
the wide new sheets with no rules, so white they'd glow,
our crayons setting out wherever we wanted to go.

Meals on Greenwood

No gumbo with its trinity
of onion, green pepper, and celery.

No lowered heads,
no grace was said.

Steak, fries, and salad at
the dining-room table with place mats

on Sunday instead of in the kitchen
was a sort of tradition—

thicker napkins, softer voices a trace
of God in our house.

Learning That Gramps Once Played the Piano

His music I knew was the jingle of change, the flat
staccato of his hammer on a nail,
the rhythmic rustling of his *Wall Street Journal*
between his spread hands when we'd visit,
the dirge of stock prices, melody of corporate
names like Procter and Gamble, Bell and Howell,
his beer-bottle's tap on the glass kitchen table
at his place at lunch, dull clinking as he sought
some screw or bolt in the basement's cluttered drawers.
I can't imagine his bent, gnarled hands at all
on the delicate keys, his feet in those torn brown slippers
glued to the ottoman lightly stepping the pedals.
But his hush during Lawrence Welk, eyes closed in the wing-chair
when *he* came on—his favorite Irish tenor.

Childhood House

We stand a long time, looking at a distance,
keeping back on the sidewalk as if behind
the rope in a museum, amazed to find
the owners haven't done any work on it since
my father sold it: our same yellow address
peeling away on the brown wooden sign
he painted himself, the now-curled shingles his hand
hammered one weekend, the same front shutters, clean once.

Somehow it survived the encroaching concrete,
thirty years of change, the whole place
almost intact between these huge new mansions
like some exhibit, and there's my brother's face
in his upstairs window, looking down again
on willow, dirt path, an orchard across the street.

Outboard Motor

After my father unhooded it, lugged it down
the steep path to the boat and clamped it on,
drew back the cord again and again like a pitch
about to be thrown, grimacing with each
whining refusal, and muttered, finally said
She doesn't want to start, after it always did,
and we shoved away from the pier, rowed out of the dense
tangle of weeds and lily pads, not once
did our resting oars uncross their feet,
not even as we entered the shallow inlet
between our lake and the next, just purring through
the reeds in that narrow passage, over the billow
of silt, the rocks, never getting stuck before
we flew through the waves, his hand guiding the tiller.

The Yellow Phone

That phone I was too old for, snuck
home in a bag from the drugstore, its cheap
yellow plastic—so thin, almost buckling
under my touch as I eased it each

day after school from my dresser drawer
to my bed, the weightless receiver attached
by a curly fake cord, those holes going nowhere,
only a vague impression that reached

wherever I wished, the clear dial that jingled
weakly as it spun (an anemic tricycle bell)
at the will of my finger, the numbers just wrinkled
misplaced stickers, but always the thrill

of calling the Beatles, a new crush, an ancient
king or queen, of crossing through
to some house in the future or dialing a distant
planet, the long crackle, wondering who

would answer, that magic phone connected
to nothing but the air, that hollow toy
you found with my socks but never said
a word about and I wish that I

had back tonight, I'd press the soft
receiver to my ear, I'd slowly spin
a hundred zeroes, then hear you lift
a piece of your cloud, call me *honey* again.

Fourth-Grade Assignment

Trying to describe herself,
she searches the catalogs' adjectives,
scans the news for words she believes
define her at nine and a half.

Carefully, to the light, she holds up
each page with boldfaced print that exclaims
who she is, or almost seems,
before her purple scissors snip.

Into her ziplock bag go words
like *fun, nice, great,* and *cool,*
then *interesting, thoughtful, dependable,*
the ones I help her find.

At the table, she arranges and glues
her chosen strips to the big paper ME,
pressing them finally down to dry,
scowling as she does

each night now at her image
in the bathroom mirror, doing her lifelong
homework that needs no cutting or gluing,
squinting into the wordless page.

Two Cents toward My Reincarnation

I hope I'm not a hawk,
hunting alone,
still watchman on a wire
above the highway's drone,
a silent single wingspan
adrift on the wind
in the open afternoon.

I'd rather, please,
be one of these
clamoring geese
passing over now, always
heading somewhere,
a member of a band
in five different keys.

The Lilac Tree

Crowded by the tulip poplar, the maple and redbud,
the lilac bush I planted to replace
those two I loved in my childhood backyard
each year grows taller, more slim, as it forces
upward for light, now waving beyond
my nose and memory, the bounds of a vase,
one high and brief pale-purple bouquet
every April as it rises away.

On Butterfield Road

After the rows of palaces rising
where cornfields swayed, the concrete drives
like roads themselves to four-car garages
the size of houses, there's only this
one red shack that keeps on
flapping in the blowing weeds,
a pickup parked in the yard, the leaning
poles of a clothesline, someone's need
still left before the stoplight, waving
in the wind they've yet to pave.

The Guard

At woods-end we hear
the grind and roar. See
toothed shovels forcing
soft green into chunked
brown rubble—three
bulldozers shoving
field into mall.

But this egret still
standing in its pond,
unruffled by the rumbling wheels,
staring into blue air,
locked there
in its thin white uniform.

Houdini's Girl

My old black shelter dog of uncertain age
and guessed-at breed, when we first brought her here,
would escape our own or any borrowed cage.
Locked tight when we'd leave, she'd greet us at the door,
wagging us back from shopping or the pool,
all teeth and fur in place. No kennel I'd fit
with wires or bungee cords could ever fool
her desire to be free, and once, when she was late
to astound us again at our entrance, I glimpsed how she
collapsed herself and slipped through the bars with ease.
I've always liked to think she's half-coyote,
and more and more, as her legs thin, muzzle grays,
she paces the house, unseen when we return,
already planning her way out of the urn.

Yard Work

Since two springs ago, the coat
of cicadas it wore for months in the swarm,
its final exhaustion, the reluctant mercy
of my lopper, the Persian lilac
remains a brittle six-inch stick.

But the Prairiefire crabapple that withered
in last year's drought, that I assumed
was dead too, hacked at in a fit
of anger over something else,
now rises back, the dark-red flames
of its leaves like hands uplifted
against my own, summoning down
these endless rains.

Beauty

It's how this glass vase isn't content
to be bound by certainty, how its different
stripes of rust and gold and pale lime-green
wind up the round body unevenly, how just one
braver wisp of gold-tinged white keeps
climbing on its own, then thins and sweeps
away into the blank future, the clear wide
neck of cerulean blue. And how my daughter cried
into her clasped hands that one night after
nearly two years, finally saying no more
to the vise-grip of her boyfriend, casting off
gray sweats to the floor, releasing a long-held laugh
as she paused, pulled free a single piece
of her tied-back hair to dangle, sweep her face.

Questions to an Atheist Daughter

Why be in such a hurry to define
yourself just yet, to paint a thick black line
around your thoughts the way you paint your eyes?
Is it worth the loss of friends, your growing loneliness,
or the classroom gasps and whispers, hallway looks
to give yourself a name? Aren't your books
enough to lug without some label too?
At lunch now they're saying you're hell-bound, calling you
a bad person; can you blame me for my worry
as you gather your folders this morning, get dressed, already
sharpening your sermon? For my talismans—
two hugs, a good-bye I dust with nonchalance?
For damning you myself when afternoon
arrives again, my tired imagination
can't find you at your locker, on the bus,
my insufficient will won't reach across
this town to silence you or make them hear?
Or see that when it's four o'clock, the door
refuses once more to budge at my command,
I'm the one each day who has to bend
my beliefs, praying and making my bargains,
bringing you home whatever way I can?

The Lawn down the Street

Each summer week it grows
more defiant, the grass
getting longer, refusing the buzz
and snap of an edger, a mower's clockwork
revs and roars, ignoring the city's
posted warnings, its only ambition
to be a field, two red-winged blackbirds
loitering all day, rough purple gangs
of wildflowers dancing as it blasts
its boom box of silence.

The Leader

After her walking partner died,
my other dog would only go
in one direction, pulling me down
the route she chose, each day the same
path past the townhouses, then around
the church, determined—snout up, just staring
ahead in her surge, ignoring my grief
for the absent alpha-dog, my efforts to turn her
toward a different scene, restrain the fragile
hips she'd had since birth, the quivering
spindles of her back legs trailing
her front ones grown powerful through the years
and now in charge.

The Grackle

Would I be like her,
who couldn't find her place
in the maple yesterday, pacing
long after we'd bagged the hatchling and mowed,
her panicked squawk through dinner, TV,
exhausting into dark,

who now, in light's return, stays
clamped to a branch exactly
above its fall, through a meal of green
wings in her beak, clucks her steady
delusional call.

Pet Shop Crow

Here, in the constant summer of the thermostat,
glassed in and not for sale, a plaque that tells
the facts of your diet and call, your habitat,
as though you were extinct or exotic, so still
and silent on your plaster branch maybe
you're stuffed and lacquered, just an educational
fake, too dark beside the yellow party
of finches, too plain against the cockatoo's frill.

But there's your tin bowl, some patio grass they've nailed
to your wall, this green square you've pecked at, frayed,
smudged back to the real color of a field,
and now, as though a button was pressed, the switchblade
of your voice, slashing the register's ring
as you unzip the black jacket of your wings.

Wood Thrush

Someone hiding, lost
long ago in these woods, voice

a glass piccolo's trickling tune
through the early-morning hush

of the birches and tamaracks, there—
behind this one, now that, calling

follow me against your straight
and heavy steps.

The Bears on Taft Street

One stands in wicker welcome at
a front door, smiling on the step,
holding up a blue-and-white pennant,
wearing a blue-and-white team cap.

Another has no body, the brown
whimsy of a resin face
and resin paws, nailed around
a tree in imagined climbing chase

of victim or prey, while forever a third
haplessly straddles a honeyless hive,
hanging from a branch, the size of a bird,
over the tamed lawn, the still river of the drive.

Tigers at the Feline Rescue Center

It's afternoon, so most just stretch and yawn
on hammered scaffolding in the late-March sun.
Around them, water vats and balls lie still.
We're told to watch for suddenly lifted tails,
to stay in single file, an arm's length away
from the cages, but all is languid tranquility,
and one our guide gets finally to chuff
hello for us has quickly had enough,
falls back to silence, licking her massive paws.

We've missed this morning's plunge of teeth and claws
into raw cow-heads, flanks hooked and thrown
through guillotine doors that swiftly shut again,
a swipe or lunge at visitors through the fence
by Sophie or Max, Rajah, Pearl, or Venus,
set free from someone's whim or childhood desire,
from circus wagons, whips, and rings of fire,
from backyard zoos, the meth dealer who needed
no guns or knives, whose customers always paid.

The Visitation

A glance, and there it is—atop
the very edge of our wooden fence,
perched as if by nail or clip,
holding on with perfect balance:

the dimmed outline of its head
without a neck, a wide dome
seeming to stare straight ahead
then turning, wings unhinging from

the huge body—its heavy, slow
rise but facile slice across
the yard with only a flap or two,
low-sweeping into darkness.

Who, sleepless, at another window
will see it next by accident?
And what, out crawling the night right now,
will feel its swift descent?

Fledgling

All morning I watch the first robin-chick out
of the nest stand balanced on the crook of my downspout,
too big to go back now, but not ready to fly,
and wonder how long the uncertain sway
of its legs can hold on to a slick five-inch
strip of aluminum, my worry must perch
next to it while the mother flits back
and forth with food for the others still tucked
in the raveling donut against my porch.

And when I see later it's gone, and my search
can't find it panicking in the grass,
I think of how quickly my mother said yes
when I flew from college, doubts and fears
packed in my suitcase, and stayed five years
tucked in her townhouse, making half
an attempt at my life, and wish she'd left
me teetering just a little bit longer
over a thornbush, below the blue air.

Hospital Room

The pleated curtains always drawn, there's no
day or night, no sun or wind, no rain.
The ever-cheerful nurses come and go
on their different shifts, their name-tagged names
and faces becoming indistinguishable.
And everything is either beige or white.
As though you're in a Pizza Hut, it's possible
to be anywhere, in any town or state.
The endless tangle of cords and tubes, the eternal
IV ticking, clacking until it beeps.
Distant chatter, fluorescence from the hall.
You watch TV for hours or stare or sleep,
waiting for the world to return its browns
and greens, its dark and light, its softer sounds.

Confession as We Argue

Each time I must agree with that woman who
years ago in the office when someone asked her casually
if she had it to do all over again would she
become a mother, paused, then smiling, said no—
next life she'd choose to travel instead, to go
wherever she pleased, to simply roam and see
the places she never could with the constant duty
of having a child—each time I think *no* too
and picture something else while you're standing there
hissing at me in defiance again, the peace
of some cabin I might have reached instead of here
on this couch as you curse away, I blink before
you're just a stubborn blur in the lake's stillness,
a nagging absence in the quiet of the pines.

Three Days before You Turn Eighteen

You'll still be here in your bed when the hour hand
slips past twelve in the dark with no sound.
Stuffed penguin will still be staring from your pillow,
the dog, unaware of a change, wedged next to you.
It will be as if we're on one
of our trips, crossing from Illinois to Wisconsin,
the same landscape on either side, the shift marked only
by a welcome sign—your cards and gifts this Sunday.
Mother. That name can never be exiled,
and my worry can stay, and I can still be called
your friend as much as we both believe.
But *Guardian,* hallowed piece of me, long before you leave
this house yourself, in three days, must shake
out her reluctant wings, heave off at midnight's stroke.

Tattoo

The pierced ears you demanded at six and I
finally gave in to, taking you to the mall
where you sat for the gun, its thud, more still
than for any shot. And all of our battles each day
over the nose stud that had to be
redone, the third ear-piercing, the gauges I assailed,
the belly-button ring you wrangled in a deal,
for two weeks doing your homework determinedly.

No longer needing permission, my signature,
you walk through the door with it tonight—
little symbols of us on the back of your shoulder
like two paisley swirls, graceful and lithe,
bowing and reaching in black ink, forever
there on your skin, in a dance we've gotten right.

Bedtime Story

Once, when you were small, afraid
to sleep alone, we moved your bed

into my room, to be right there,
and we slept for months like sisters:

both of us brushed, tucked in by eight,
saying good night, but not ready yet

to close our eyes, still softly talking
across the space of dark between

our parallel edges as we drifted off,
voices a thinning bridge, and you knew for that brief

time in your childhood the night a little less
deep and vast.

The Church on Woodlawn

The ever-changing sign today
says *The Vineyard Church,* last month's
brief identity painted away,
along with all the others once:
Alliance, Woodlawn Community, and
Healing Rivers Revival Center,
though a single man-made pond
is the only hint of water near.
And now no sign of grapes or arbor,
only the crumbling lot that needs
revival itself, the double doors
once red, now blue, the congregating weeds,
the white sides starting to peel, and still
atop the steeple, robed in rust,
no matter the wind, the year, an angel
weather-vane always pointing west,
her flightless, hammered wings, the raised
mute horn she forever blows, a herald
naming our final, eternal place
whatever this lost church is called.

Preparations

Through constant binoculars you watch
the birds' habits, how they work
back and forth from the lakeside patch
of trees to your feeders. With bifocals perched

you study field guides on their lives,
know this one's song, what that one eats,
field or woodland where it thrives.
And I collect evidence with each

summer's visit: a few more lost
teeth, your thinning voice and hair,
bags of sunflower seeds, tossed
husks on the table, around your chair.

Back home, I theorize, imagine
how you spend your nights alone:
standing there on the deck of your cabin,
whistling your chosen tune,

getting ready to embark,
your arms practicing in the vast dark.

Tulip

Every spring, looking
out my window I find it
standing like a small girl
in the garden behind my house,
the only one, rising
each year from a magic bulb
through the weeds and dirt, planted
by someone who lived here before me.

In her last autumn she
hunches to the soil,
her body thin as a stem,
green coat flapping
in the October wind, the back
of her pink-scarfed head.

Garden at the Condos

Too small yet to see past it,
the parking lot and cars,
the dull brick buildings where we live,
to notice the rusted dumpster

three feet away, oblivious
to last night's bottle caps and shards,
tossed cigarette butts, through the thinnest
door through the coneflowers my daughter enters

and drifts each afternoon with the bees
in a pink and yellow field that blooms
right *here,* the fast-food wrappers these
decorations on the stems.

The Service

The minister at the podium
stammered through the dates and events
of my grandfather's life from a xeroxed sheet
someone, last minute, had handed him.

As he squinted over the typos
in his sliding glasses, tight suit of a clown,
changing decades and places, no one
could keep from snickering, rolling eyes.

And when he listed the family, misread
my aunt's last name as a first, adding
a grandson called George, I almost burst,
my father groaned and shook his head.

But when he reached the end of the paper,
began to sing of the higher place
he was going—my grandfather, who praised
numbers and facts, on Sundays went nowhere

but his own back-porch—I saw him lifting
in the checkered wing-chair, feet still propped
on the ottoman as further and further up
he soared, then slowly floated down

to a cloud at the back, his beer and cashews
fixed on a wispy sill, and he
behind the *Wall Street Journal*, eternally
praying for his stocks to rise.

Night Exposure

We pose the old camera up on the tripod
and open the portal of its eye
as wide as we can, setting the shutter
for one whole minute.

Then freeze ourselves so we don't leave
those blurs, called ghosts, on the picture, clenching
smiles and locking elbows together,
now holding our breath at the click.

What will happen as we stand
so still in these sixty seconds stretched,
trying not to laugh or blink,
almost forgetting to feel?
Will the print reveal
only a dark blank?

Or will it be as someone said:
we'll see them scattered in the spaces
they never really left, the dead
there on the deck, a few by that tree,
some smiling behind us, more at our shoulders,
like stars come out.

Song from Town

There's a constancy here I like:
how each cat stretches out on its own
driveway, the one it knows.

And how each Monday morning all
the trash cans down the street create
two long and neat receding rows.

My neighbor to the left
I can count on always to hand me
a Bud Light when he pulls in.

The back-and-forth tap
of ping-pong paddles that happens on
the porch of my neighbors to the right

after their daughter is back from school
I remember. At ten o'clock I'm sure
those shrieks from the two little girls who

moved in across the street twelve
years too late, who run to bubbles
their mother sets free, will last exactly

half an hour. I'm still not quite
used to Regina yelling at Bill
through their sliding-glass door behind me at

seven a.m. as he bangs in the shed,
then drowns her out with the leaf blower.
But the east light always hits my

swirled bottles on the west-wall
shelf just right, and the west comes
through where it should to make glow

two flasks from the 1800s. And,
though I yearned for a house in the country,
far from anyone, on a nameless road,

a mailbox I'd walk to, then back from,
a driveway of grass, the only banging
door my own,

I've almost, almost begun to love
each day the hum of a mower going
at any time, all day long.

Elise Hempel was born in Evanston, Illinois, and grew up in suburban Chicago. She received her BA and MA from Eastern Illinois University, and she has worked as an editor, proofreader, copywriter and university English instructor. Her poems have appeared in numerous journals, including *Poetry, Measure, Valparaiso Poetry Review, The Evansville Review,* and *The Midwest Quarterly,* as well as in Ted Kooser's weekly column, *American Life in Poetry.* She is the recipient of an Illinois Arts Council Literary Award and the winner of the 2015 *Able Muse* Write Prize in Poetry, and has been a finalist or semifinalist for several book awards. In 2014 her chapbook, *Only Child,* was published by Finishing Line Press. She lives in central Illinois.

Second Rain was a finalist for the 2015 Able Muse Book Award.

ALSO FROM ABLE MUSE PRESS

William Baer, *Times Square and Other Stories*

Melissa Balmain, *Walking in on People – Poems*

Ben Berman, *Strange Borderlands – Poems*

Ben Berman, *Figuring in the Figure – Poems*

Michael Cantor,
　Life in the Second Circle – Poems

Catherine Chandler, *Lines of Flight – Poems*

William Conelly, *Uncontested Grounds – Poems*

Maryann Corbett,
　*Credo for the Checkout Line in Winter –
　Poems*

John Philip Drury, *Sea Level Rising – Poems*

D.R. Goodman, *Greed: A Confession – Poems*

Margaret Ann Griffiths,
　Grasshopper – The Poetry of M A Griffiths

Katie Hartsock, *Bed of Impatiens – Poems*

Jan D. Hodge, *Taking Shape – carmina figurata*

Ellen Kaufman, *House Music – Poems*

Emily Leithauser, *The Borrowed World – Poems*

Carol Light, *Heaven from Steam – Poems*

April Lindner,
　This Bed Our Bodies Shaped – Poems

Martin McGovern, *Bad Fame – Poems*

Jeredith Merrin, *Cup – Poems*

Richard Newman,
　All the Wasted Beauty of the World – Poems

Alfred Nicol, *Animal Psalms – Poems*

Frank Osen, *Virtue, Big as Sin – Poems*

Alexander Pepple (Editor),
　Able Muse Anthology

Alexander Pepple (Editor),
　Able Muse – a review of poetry, prose & art
　(semiannual issues, Winter 2010 onward)

James Pollock, *Sailing to Babylon – Poems*

Aaron Poochigian, *The Cosmic Purr – Poems*

John Ridland,
　*Sir Gawain and the Green Knight –
　Translation*

Stephen Scaer, *Pumpkin Chucking – Poems*

Hollis Seamon, *Corporeality – Stories*

Carrie Shipers, *Cause for Concern – Poems*

Matthew Buckley Smith,
　Dirge for an Imaginary World – Poems

Barbara Ellen Sorensen,
　*Compositions of the Dead Playing Flutes –
　Poems*

Wendy Videlock,
　Slingshots and Love Plums – Poems

Wendy Videlock,
　The Dark Gnu and Other Poems

Wendy Videlock, *Nevertheless – Poems*

Richard Wakefield, *A Vertical Mile – Poems*

Gail White, *Asperity Street – Poems*

Chelsea Woodard, *Vellum – Poems*

www.ablemusepress.com

www.ingramcontent.com/pod-product-compliance
Lightning Source LLC
Chambersburg PA
CBHW022152090426
42742CB00010B/1486